CHERRY WOOD'S DISCOVERY

ABC'S

DR. JOYCE MARRIE

ILLUSTRATED by
OGBRU EVIDENCE

Chloe
Arts
And
Publishing, LLC
write the vision make it plain, Habakkuk 2:2

Library of Congress 1-11460691641
ISBN 979-8-9891993-1-0
First Edition
Chloe Arts Publishing, LLC
Printed in the United States

To my Stella a shining "Star"

Aa

APPLE

Bb

BANANA

Cc

CAT

Dd

DOG

E e

ELEPHANT

Ff

FOX

Gg

GOAT

Hh

HORSE

Ii

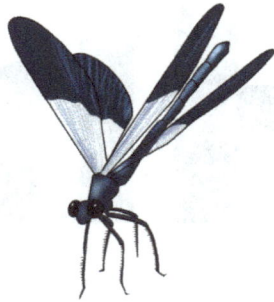

INSECT

Jj

JELLY FISH

Kk

KITE

Ll

LOG

Mm

MAN

Nn

NUTS

Oo

OWL

Pp

PEARS

Qq

QUAIL

Rr

RAIN

Ss

SUN

Tt

TREE

Uu

UMBRELLA

Vv

VEGETABLE

Ww

WHALE

Xx

XYLOPHONE

Yy

YAK

Zz

ZEBRA

MORE BOOK OFFERS:
Cherry Wood Learns about Juneteenth - Cherry Wood Finds a Home - Cherry Wood is Happy Again! - Cherry Wood's Birthday Celebration

FOR MORE INFORMATION CONTACT:
 https://chloeartsandpublishing.com
https://cherrywooddoll.com
Cherry Wood Doll is a registered trademark of Cherry Wood Series

www.ingramcontent.com/pod-product-compliance
Lightning Source LLC
Chambersburg PA
CBHW050216270326
41914CB00003BA/443